"Successful people do what unsuccessful people are not willing to do." —Jim Rohn

Did you start your business to build a better life for you and your family? Is your reality that you are working so much, you aren't spending any time with your family or when you are with them, you are so stressed out over the business that they kind of wish you weren't there?

What would it be like if you could **experience the financial abundance you desire, without the stress of a complicated and consuming business?**

This is exactly why I've created the Decisive Business Assessment. You will be amazed what you will learn about your business in just four minutes. After taking the assessment, you will receive a summary of your results and important next steps for you.

Take the assessment at
http://DecisiveAssessment.com.

Michele Scism on the Rules of Effective Content Marketing

Why Your Content Marketing Execution Is Your Social Proof

Michele Scism

THiNKaha®

An Actionable Business Journal

E-mail: info@thinkaha.com
20660 Stevens Creek Blvd., Suite 210
Cupertino, CA 95014

Published by THiNKaha®
20660 Stevens Creek Blvd., Suite 210, Cupertino, CA 95014
http://thinkaha.com
E-mail: info@thinkaha.com

First Printing: September 2018
Hardcover ISBN: 978-1-61699-278-1 1-61699-278-6
Paperback ISBN: 978-1-61699-277-4 1-61699-277-8
eBook ISBN: 978-1-61699-276-7 1-61699-276-X
Place of Publication: Silicon Valley, California, USA
Paperback Library of Congress Number: 2018909378

Trademarks

All terms mentioned in this book that are known to be trademarks or service marks have been appropriately capitalized. Neither THiNKaha, nor any of its imprints, can attest to the accuracy of this information. Use of a term in this book should not be regarded as affecting the validity of any trademark or service mark.

Warning and Disclaimer

Every effort has been made to make this book as complete and as accurate as possible. The information provided is on an "as is" basis. The author(s), publisher, and their agents assume no responsibility for errors or omissions. Nor do they assume liability or responsibility to any person or entity with respect to any loss or damages arising from the use of information contained herein.

Dedication

This book is dedicated to the men and women who call themselves entrepreneurs. You are the backbone of the economy. You employ a huge part of the population and thus, have a major impact on families and their future success. Thank you for having the courage to do what you do!

Acknowledgement

I would like to acknowledge Mitchell Levy and the entire team at AHAthat. Thank you for believing in the power of content and the entrepreneur's dream.

How to Read a THiNKaha® Book
A Note from the Publisher

The AHAthat/THiNKaha series is the CliffsNotes of the 21st century. These books are contextual in nature. Although the actual words won't change, their meaning will every time you read one as your context will change. Be ready, you will experience your own AHA moments as you read the AHA messages™ in this book. They are designed to be stand-alone actionable messages that will help you think about a project you're working on, an event, a sales deal, a personal issue, etc. differently. As you read this book, please think about the following:

1. It should only take 15-20 minutes to read this book the first time out. When you're reading, write in the underlined area one to three action items that resonate with you.
2. Mark your calendar to re-read this book again in 30 days.
3. Repeat step #1 and mark one to three more AHA messages that resonate. They will most likely be different than the first time. BTW: this is also a great time to reflect on the AHAmessages that resonated with you during your last reading.

After reading a THiNKaha book, marking your AHA messages, re-reading it, and marking more AHA messages, you'll begin to see how these books contextually apply to you. AHAthat/THiNKaha books advocate for continuous, lifelong learning. They will help you transform your AHAs into actionable items with tangible results until you no longer have to say AHA to these moments—they'll become part of your daily practice as you continue to grow and learn.

Mitchell Levy, The AHA Guy at AHAthat
publisher@thinkaha.com

THiNKaha®

Contents

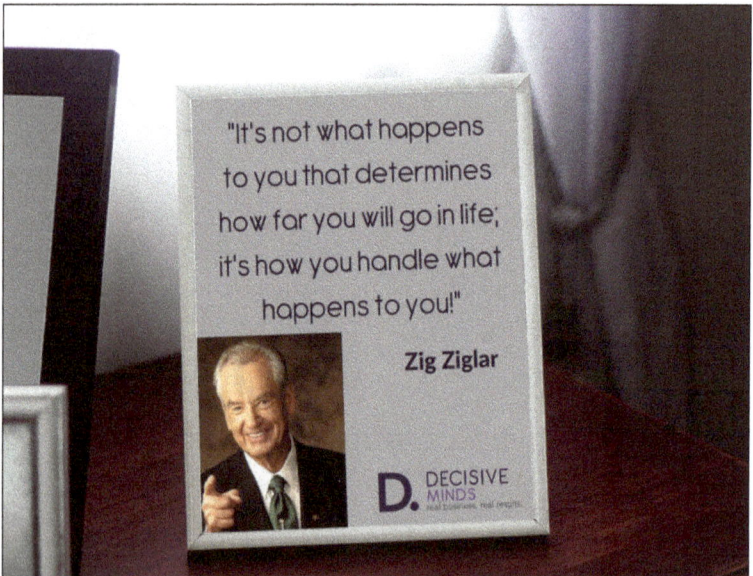

Share the AHA messages from this book socially by going to
http://aha.pub/EffectiveContentMarketing.

Section I
The Proper Mindset

In a world where social media plays a big role in the lives of many, people usually decide on what to buy or whom to buy from based on information they find online or recommendations of friends.

Many entrepreneurs are attempting to build their online reputation by becoming known through social media, blogging, and video sites. When you post online, you are using a strategy called content marketing. Although it may feel like you can just post whatever you want throughout the day, an effective content marketing strategy requires a strategic implementation plan and mental commitment.

This is not only to stop feeding your fear of missing out on this opportunity but also to help customers move through the process of knowing, liking, and trusting your business. Change in business is inevitable, and to keep up as an entrepreneur, you need to change the way you look at online content marketing.

Watch this video: http://aha.pub/ECMs1.

1

Read Michele Scism on the Rules of
#EffectiveContentMarketing.
http://aha.pub/EffectiveContentMarketing
@ResultsLady

_____

_____

_____

2

Change in business is inevitable.
Don't fight it. The next step leads to the next
big picture. #EffectiveContentMarketing
@ResultsLady

_____

_____

_____

3

Business has changed. Have you?
#EffectiveContentMarketing
@ResultsLady https://decisiveminds.com/

_____

_____

_____

4

People are willing to buy things because
they've been told 100 times that they need
to buy them. #ConvertibleContent
@ResultsLady

_____

_____

_____

5

Entrepreneurs have the tendency to see the opportunity in everything. What should you do? #EffectiveContentMarketing @ResultsLady

_____

_____

_____

6

Know where all the pieces fit in the plan, what pieces you're going to keep, and what you're going to stop doing. @ResultsLady

_____

_____

_____

7

Purposefully build your online reputation so people can find you. #BeSeenAndGetFound #EffectiveContentMarketing @ResultsLady

_____

_____

_____

8

Watch people online who are making money. If they're making money, you can too! #PositiveWins #EffectiveContentMarketing @ResultsLady

---

9

Use #EffectiveContentMarketing to help people move through the process of knowing, liking, and trusting your business. @ResultsLady

_____

_____

_____

10

Social Media has changed the way we build relationships and the way we make buying decisions. #EffectiveContentMarketing @ResultsLady

_____

_____

_____

11

Over the last 12 to 15 years, business has completely changed how it operates and what customers expect from them. @ResultsLady

_____

_____

_____

12

People take action because of FOMO: #FearOfMissingOut. #SocialProofMatters @ResultsLady

_____

_____

_____

13

Don't assume everyone knows what
you know. We all have knowledge
that other people don't know about.
#ShareWhatYouKnow @ResultsLady

_____

_____

_____

14

Successful content marketing requires
an implementation plan and your
commitment. #EffectiveContentMarketing
@ResultsLady

_____

_____

_____

Share the AHA messages from this book socially by going to
http://aha.pub/EffectiveContentMarketing.

Section II
The Value of Online Presence and Social Proof

Nowadays, it is essential to create an online presence to increase the value of your company. Social media platforms such as Facebook, LinkedIn, Twitter and Instagram are worldwide venues where you can find prospects without spending millions. Social media is the great equalizer that allows small business owners to compete with major brands in their market.

When you create your online content, you must stick to your own values, since your online presence represents your business. The goal of online content is to get your prospect to visit your website, build a relationship with you, and ultimately purchase your products and services.

To accomplish this, you should create content on your website and social media that speaks to what your audience is already searching for on Google and other search engines. Remember, people do things because they see others doing them. That is social proof. So, the more people begin to interact, share, comment, and recommend your content, the more their friends will pay attention.

Watch this video: http://aha.pub/ECMs2.

15

You had better figure out how to get your business seen online. Your competion is figuring it out. #EffectiveContentMarketing @ResultsLady

_____

_____

_____

16

Being online is one of the components of building your business. Is your business online? #EffectiveContentMarketing @ResultsLady

_____

_____

_____

17

Use your online presence to find prospects to have in-person conversations with. #EffectiveContentMarketing @ResultsLady

_____

_____

_____

18

Creating an online presence is a necessity to increase the value of your company. #EffectiveContentMarketing @ResultsLady

_____

_____

_____

19

Remember, you get to design how
your online presence represents
your business. Stick to your values!
#EffectiveContentMarketing @ResultsLady

_____

_____

_____

20

Use your website to share content that gets you ranked and seen by Google and other search engines. #AimToBeSeen @ResultsLady

_____

_____

_____

21

When somebody hears your name, the first thing they do is search you on Google. #BeSearchable #EffectiveContentMarketing @ResultsLady

_____

_____

_____

22

Social Media has leveled the playing field. Small businesses can now market to massive audiences without spending millions. @ResultsLady

_____

_____

_____

23

One of the main reasons for #SocialMediaMarketing is to be seen and to encourage people to get to know you. #EffectiveContent @ResultsLady

_____

_____

_____

24

Use social media and content marketing to expand your audience of people who know, like, and trust you. #EffectiveContent @ResultsLady

_____

_____

_____

25

Social media and content marketing has given people who don't have money to spend on ads and TV commercials a chance. @ResultsLady

_____

_____

_____

26

Every person is now able to market themselves, thanks to social media and content marketing. #EffectiveContentMarketing @ResultsLady

_____

_____

_____

27

"15,000 people like her, so I'm probably going to like her too." That's #SocialProof @ResultsLady

_____

_____

_____

28

Facebook knows you are more likely to do something because your friends did — that's called social proof. #ContentMarketing @ResultsLady

_____

_____

_____

29

Your content marketing execution is
your social proof. Are you controlling it?
#EffectiveContentMarketing @ResultsLady

_____

_____

_____

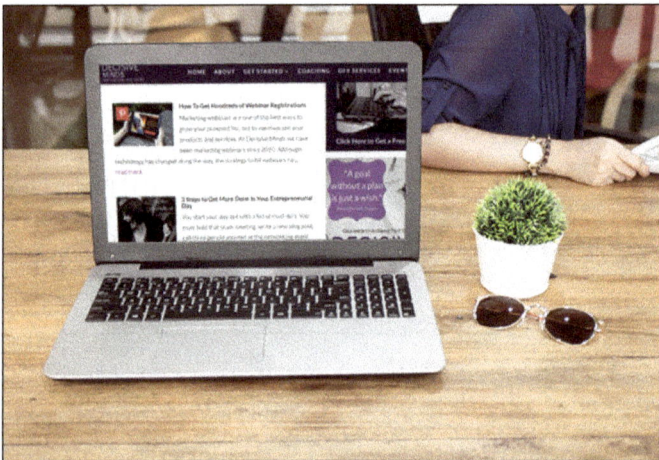

Share the AHA messages from this book socially by going to
http://aha.pub/EffectiveContentMarketing.

Section III
Content Creation

Successful businesses use effective content marketing strategies. And for many of you, just reading the words effective content marketing strategies makes you cringe. Why? Because it sounds like an overwhelming idea.

I have great news for you: content creation can be simple. Record your sales pitch, pull out the content, and use it to create blog posts, videos, and social media posts. If you have written a book or articles of any sort, content can be pulled from there to create social media posts or blog posts.

It is important to take note of how visual people are, so be sure to include lots of pictures and video in your content marketing strategy. How you package your knowledge determines the kind of business image you create in people's minds.

Watch this video: http://aha.pub/ECMs3.

30

Successful businesses put out a lot of content. Content is the currency of the online world. #EffectiveContentMarketing @ResultsLady

_____

_____

_____

31

Even if you cut grass for a living,
you've got knowledge that you
can sell. #PackageYourKnowledge
#EffectiveContent @ResultsLady

_____

_____

_____

32

To create content, you simply have to
know something about something. It's
really that simple. #YouHaveContent
#EffectiveContent @ResultsLady

_____

_____

_____

33

#Blogging and #BookWriting are formats
of content. 700 words or less is a blog.
#EffectiveContentMarketing @ResultsLady

_____

_____

_____

34

A chapter from your book makes a great series of blog posts. #InstantContent #EffectiveContentMarketing @ResultsLady

_____

_____

_____

35

Create content by recording videos or doing internet-based radio shows. @ResultsLady http://aha.pub/EffectiveContentMarketing

_____

_____

_____

36

One of the ways to create content is by being interviewed on other people's shows. #BlogTalkRadio @ResultsLady https://decisiveminds.com/

_____

_____

_____

37

Write a blog post, then record yourself
speaking it. Now you have audio as well!
#TwoForOne #RepurposeContent
@ResultsLady

_____

_____

_____

38

You can create a visual image content out of quotes from your audios. Now you've got pictures! #TwoForOne #RepurposeContent @ResultsLady

_____

_____

_____

39

Your business needs visual content because that's what grabs people's attention on #Facebook & #Google. #BeVisual #EffectiveContent @ResultsLady

_____

_____

_____

40

Content doesn't have to be all text. It can be pictures. That's #VisualContent. #EffectiveContentMarketing @ResultsLady

---

41

To turn your knowledge into an info product, start by having a friend interview you on your topic & then have that transcribed. @ResultsLady

_____

_____

_____

42

You can get 3 pieces of content from 1. Start with video, strip out the audio & have it transcribed. #Repurpose @ResultsLady

_____

_____

_____

43

How can you get 5 results out of every piece of content? Take the original piece of content and turn into a Blog, Video, Social Media Images, and webinar content.
@ResultsLady

_____

_____

_____

44

Businesses need to have visual content. You need to be able to show your story visually. #BeVisual #CreateContent @ResultsLady

_____

_____

_____

45

You're smarter than you think. Your content is in you. You just need to let it out. #EffectiveContentMarketing @ResultsLady

_____

_____

_____

46

The difference between blogging and
article writing is that articles are long,
while a blog won't exceed 700 words.
@ResultsLady

_____

_____

_____

47

One approach to getting content out is to record your sales pitch, then break that down to bites of content. #ContentMarketing @ResultsLady

_____

_____

_____

48

Every single soul on this earth
has knowledge that people will
buy. #PackageYourKnowledge
#EffectiveContentMarketing @ResultsLady

_____

_____

_____

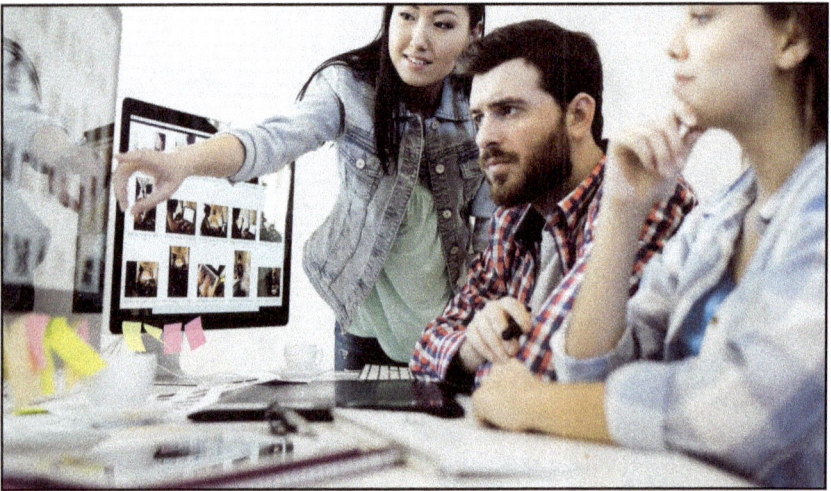

Share the AHA messages from this book socially by going to
http://aha.pub/EffectiveContentMarketing.

Section IV
Creating Your Content Marketing Strategy

A successful content marketing strategy focuses on a few methods that work best for your business. Content can be created in three ways: written, visual, and verbal. You should utilize all three in your strategy because different people like different formats of content. Is there one of these that grabs your customers' attention more often? What gets shared and liked on social media?

Sharing great content is not enough. You must also include a call-to-action. This is how you tell your customers what to do next. Your call-to-action may be for them to click on the buy button, to share your blog post on Facebook, or to simply leave a comment.

Content marketing is a tool through which you can educate your prospects and build your customers' confidence in you. Remember to plan on a couple strategies, measure results, and find which one works best.

Watch this video: http://aha.pub/ECMs4.

49

When creating an #EffectiveContentMarketing strategy, focus on a few strategies for the most results. @ResultsLady

_____

_____

_____

50

There are three big basics to content marketing: written content, visual content & verbal content. Try one or all! @ResultsLady

_____

_____

_____

51

Facebook's newsfeed changed. It expanded so the videos and images become bigger; that's how important they are. @ResultsLady

_____

_____

_____

52

#VisualContent is important because when people scroll through Facebook or other social media sites, that's where they stop. @ResultsLady

_____

_____

_____

53

Planning your #ContentStrategy? See if you can recreate content in a different format to be used elsewhere. @ResultsLady

_____

_____

_____

54

There's no one-size-fits-all
#EffectiveContentMarketing strategy.
What techniques capture your audience's
attention? @ResultsLady

_____

_____

_____

55

When you hire a #SocialMedia manager, you have to know enough to be able to tell if you're getting results. #EffectiveContent @ResultsLady

_____

_____

_____

56

A #CallToAction is an important #ContentMarketing strategy. Have one at the end of every piece of content you have. @ResultsLady

_____

_____

_____

57

A #CallToAction tells people what to do next. If you tell them what to do, they will do it. #EffectiveContentMarketing @ResultsLady

_____

_____

_____

58

With #EffectiveContentMarketing, you don't necessarily need to create new content every time. #Repurpose @ResultsLady

_____

_____

_____

59

People respond to a call to action unconsciously. Each piece of content needs a #CallToAction. #EffectiveContentMarketing @ResultsLady

_____

_____

60

When choosing a platform for #ContentMarketing, choose one that resonates not just with you but also with your prospects. @ResultsLady

_____

_____

_____

61

If you're doing #ContentMarketing
on Facebook and YouTube, you need
to track what gets shared and liked.
#KnowYourNumbers @ResultsLady

_____

_____

_____

62

For an #EffectiveContentMarketing strategy to work, you need to monitor what the interactions are and how many. @ResultsLady

_____

_____

_____

63

Everyone has a #ContentMarketingStrategy that works for them. What's yours? @ResultsLady

_____

_____

_____

64

When creating your #ContentMarketing strategy, plan on a couple tactics, measure results & finding 2-3 that work best. @ResultsLady

_____

_____

_____

65

Content marketing is the strategy to deliver info that educates prospects and builds trust. #BuildRelationships @ResultsLady

_____

_____

_____

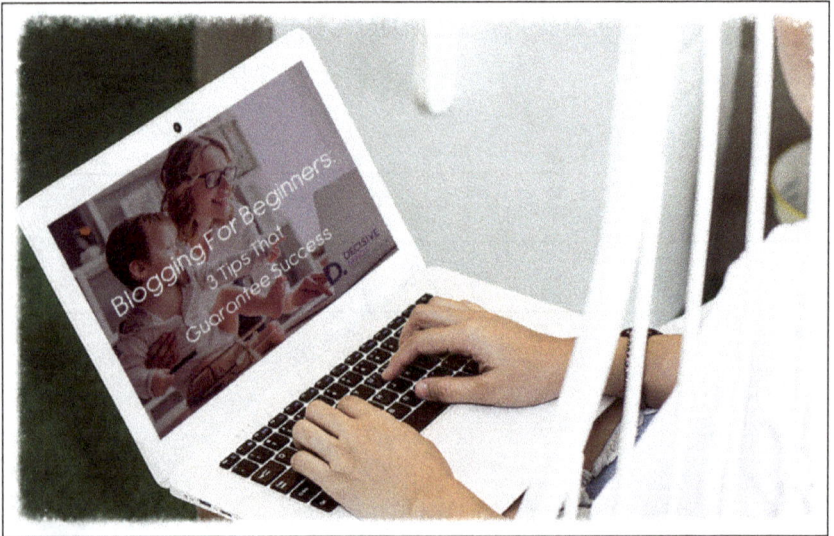

Share the AHA messages from this book socially by going to
http://aha.pub/EffectiveContentMarketing.

Section V
Ways of Effective Content Marketing

When building an effective content marketing strategy, you start by determining which platforms you will be using. Facebook pages, Facebook groups, and YouTube channels are a few of the many platforms you may use in spreading your content.

Your website is another powerful platform. Did you know that 80 percent of the activities on the web is done on mobile? It is necessary for you to create a business website that is mobile-friendly and responsive.

Webinars are also effective for content marketing. You must understand the direction you are trying to take your customers. Powerful webinars are convertible webinars, meaning that at the end of the webinar, your prospect is motivated to buy.

If content marketing is done well, it'll absolutely be a done deal. Customers and prospects will know, like, and trust you, buy from you, and refer you.

Watch this video: **http://aha.pub/ECMs5**.

66

Content marketing is the action taken to allow your prospects to know, like, and trust you. #EffectiveContentMarketing @ResultsLady

_____

_____

_____

67

Start with the basics: #Facebook pages, Facebook groups & #YouTube channels are great platforms for #EffectiveContentMarketing. @ResultsLady

_____

_____

_____

68

#EffectiveContentMarketing is all about consistency and persistence. Choose three strategies and stick to them. @ResultsLady

_____

_____

_____

69

For #EffectiveContentMarketing, you don't need to do 45 things. You just need to find a couple that work really well. @ResultsLady

_____

_____

_____

70

80% of everything done on the web is done on mobile. Your website MUST be optimized for mobile. #MobileFriendly @ResultsLady

_____

_____

_____

71

Having a website is important and having it be mobile friendly and responsive is a necessity. #EffectiveContentMarketing @ResultsLady

----

72

Webinars are an
#EffectiveContentMarketing strategy but
only if they are a convertible webinar.
#KnowYourConversion @ResultsLady

_____

_____

_____

73

To become successful in #ContentMarketing, you must drive your prospects to the "know, like, and trust" factor. @ResultsLady

_____

_____

_____

74

People make decisions after they see something about 15 to 25 times. Spread your content! #EffectiveContentMarketing @ResultsLady

_____

_____

_____

75

Effective webinar marketing means understanding what your webinar is going to drive people to. #CallToAction @ResultsLady

_____

_____

_____

76

A new speaker can get started by creating their own show or webinar series. Show off your speaking ability. @ResultsLady

_____

_____

_____

77

When putting out content, have a strategic path that ties everything together for prospects to know what to do next. @ResultsLady

_____

_____

_____

78

Content marketing can make people trust you, and people who trust you will buy from you. #EffectiveContentMarketing @ResultsLady

_____

_____

_____

79

Done right, content marketing gets your customers and prospects to know, like, and refer you. #EffectiveContentMarketing @ResultsLady

---

80

In the beginning of a #ContentMarketing strategy, you test different options to find what your audience likes. @ResultsLady

---

81

Having a #CallToAction improves your close rate. What's your close rate now? #EffectiveContentMarketing @ResultsLady

_____

_____

_____

82

#EffectiveContentMarketing makes it so
easy for your prospect to say YES.
No other option! @ResultsLady

_____

_____

_____

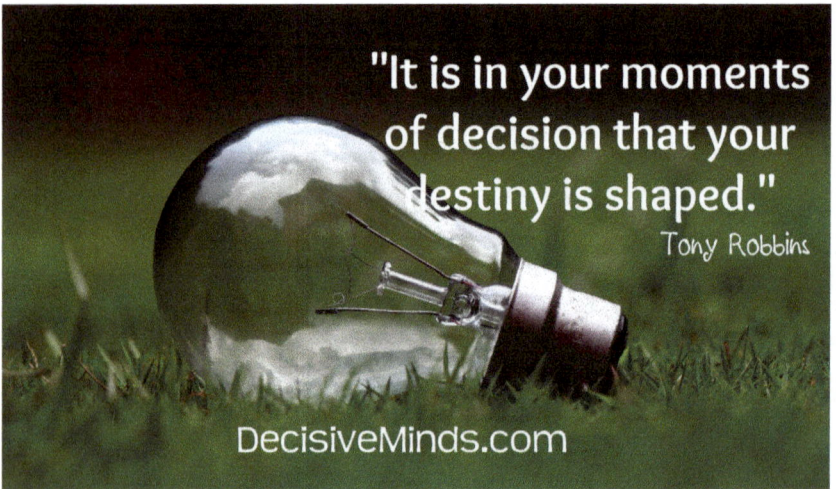

"It is in your moments of decision that your destiny is shaped."
Tony Robbins

DecisiveMinds.com

Share the AHA messages from this book socially by going to
http://aha.pub/EffectiveContentMarketing.

Section VI
Being Clear and Simple

The ultimate goal of content marketing is to build a community of people who are loyal to you, love you, and will share you. Social media is a promising medium for a business to grow, provided that systems are in place and conversations are taken to a personal level.

When creating your content, keep it simple, don't overthink it, and be keyword specific. Listen to your prospects, and use the same words they do in your content. They will be able to easily place themselves in the conversation.

Analyze your content marketing strategy and give it enough time to work. That is why it is essential to have three strategies for effective content marketing. Why? So if one of those strategies is not working, you still have the other two.

Watch this video: http://aha.pub/ECMs6.

83

Don't over-think it. Our goal is very simple: build a community of people who are loyal, love us & share us. #ContentMarketing @ResultsLady

_____

_____

_____

84

Social media is useless if you don't have your systems in place. #ListBuilding #Community #EffectiveContentMarketing @ResultsLady

_____

_____

_____

85

Create your plan & start running
toward it. If you stumble, get back
up and keep going. #MakingMoney
#EffectiveContentMarketing @ResultsLady

86

When someone loves the work you do, they
can promote you and tell others about you.
#EffectiveContentMarketing @ResultsLady

87

If you're good at building content, being keyword specific will help you drive organic traffic. #EffectiveContentMarketing @ResultsLady

_____

_____

_____

88

Attend conferences for two things:
content and context. #GrowSmallBusiness
#EffectiveContentMarketing @ResultsLady

_____

_____

_____

89

It's vital to analyze your #ContentMarketing
strategy first and give it enough time. If it's
not working, then shift. @ResultsLady

_____

_____

_____

90

You need three strategies for #EffectiveContentMarketing because if one is not working, you still have the other two. @ResultsLady

_____

_____

_____

91

Purposefully build your online reputation so people can find you. # BeSeenAndGetFound #EffectiveContentMarketing @ResultsLady

_____

_____

_____

92

There are certain numbers we need
to be looking at and tracking from an
#EffectiveContentMarketing strategy side.
@ResultsLady

_____

_____

_____

93

Create your marketing strategy around the knowledge you have, and that should determine which type of content you'll create. @ResultsLady

_____

_____

_____

94

Make what you do look so easy that others are interested in doing it themselves (or having you do it for them). @ResultsLady

_____

_____

_____

95

#SocialMediaMarketing is changing constantly. What worked yesterday may not work tomorrow. @ResultsLady

_____

_____

_____

96

Give people small, little bites that
they can absorb and do. #MakeItEasy
#EffectiveContentMarketing @ResultsLady

_____

_____

_____

97

Small Business Owners think that social media gets clients. Only true if you're taking the conversation off social media.
@ResultsLady

_____

_____

_____

98

The goal of #ContentMarketing is to build a relationship of trust between you and your prospect. #BuildTrust @ResultsLady

_____

_____

_____

99

You need to be online for people
to find you and connect with you.
#EffectiveContentMarketing @ResultsLady

_____

_____

_____

100

When looking at #ContentMarketing metrics, be careful not to jump to the conclusion that it's not working. #BePositive @ResultsLady

_____

_____

_____

" Marketing is telling the world you're a rock star. Content Marketing is showing the world you are one."

Robert Rose

DecisiveMinds.com

Share the AHA messages from this book socially by going to
http://aha.pub/EffectiveContentMarketing.

Section VII
Building the Audience You Are Going to Market To

You need to build a significant community before expecting people to take action. Know your prospects and focus on what they want, not what you think they need. Since people are looking for the information already, use it as the doorway to get their attention. Make sure to build a specific community that is attracted to you and your way of doing things—meaning that you are not looking for everyone to be part of your community.

Keep an eye on your audience size, interaction, and conversion in order to know if your content marketing is successful. Through Google Analytics, you can now check on what's a hot content topic that can help boost your interaction with your audience and eventually lead them to take action.

Watch this video: **http://aha.pub/ECMs7**.

101

An #EffectiveContentMarketing strategy focuses on who your prospect is and what they are already looking for. @ResultsLady

_____

_____

_____

102

Measure your audience size, interaction, and conversion to see your success from #EffectiveContentMarketing. @ResultsLady

_____

_____

_____

103

Find prospects by offering them what they are already looking for — not what you know they need. @ResultsLady

_____

_____

_____

104

#SocialMedia interactions should lead to actions. Like clicking on a link to your sales page or video. #EffectiveContent @ResultsLady

_____

_____

_____

105

If you've been in an industry for 20 years, you have 20 years of jargon. Be careful not to use it. #EffectiveContentMarketing @ResultsLady

_____

_____

_____

106

If a third grader can't understand what you're doing or saying, you're not doing it right. #MakeItEasy #EffectiveContent @ResultsLady

_____

_____

_____

107

Bad reviews happen. Don't let it stop you. If you put out a lot of great content, the bad reviews will not matter. @ResultsLady

_____

_____

_____

108

It is important that people know who you are because this is the first step for them to trust you. #EffectiveContent @ResultsLady

_____

_____

_____

109

The whole process of content marketing is build your audience & build relationship. Is your audience growing? #EffectiveContent @ResultsLady

_____

_____

_____

110

Get your prospect's attention by
giving them what they are already
looking for. That's your doorway.
#EffectiveContentMarketing @ResultsLady

_____

_____

_____

111

Remember, your #ContentMarketing must be about what your prospects want — not what you know they need. @ResultsLady

_____

_____

_____

112

Some online lurkers will eventually step out of their corner & interact with your business. Encourage it! #EffectiveContent @ResultsLady

_____

_____

_____

113

People build their own relationship with you through your content without you ever knowing. #ConnectingWithContent @ResultsLady

_____

_____

_____

114

Because people are looking for the info already, use it as the door to get their attention. #UseADoorway @ResultsLady

_____

_____

_____

115

There will come a point where expanding your community becomes a very natural thing. #BePersistent #EffectiveContent @ResultsLady

---

116

Using #ContentMarketing to expand your audience of people who know, like, and trust you can help your business greatly. @ResultsLady

---

117

You need to build a significant enough community before expecting people to take action. #KeepBuilding #EffectiveContent @ResultsLady

_____

_____

_____

118

Google gives you the ability to hone in on your prospects so that your #ContentMarketing is more effective. @ResultsLady

———————————————————

———————————————————

———————————————————

119

What's the question your prospect has already that you can answer? That's your door. Go for it. #EffectiveContentMarketing @ResultsLady

———————————————————

———————————————————

———————————————————

120

Build a specific community that is attracted to you and your way of doing things. #EffectiveContentMarketing @ResultsLady

_____

_____

_____

121

We each have a unique community. Although we might both be working with entrepreneurs, we're attracting different prospects. @ResultsLady

_____

_____

_____

122

Use #GoogleAnalytics to determine your content topics. Google is very smart; they know more about us than we know about them. @ResultsLady

_____

_____

_____

123

60% of people will follow and watch you but won't interact because they're too scared. #EffectiveContentMarketing @ResultsLady

_____

_____

_____

124

Most people online are lurkers and build their own relationship with you without ever speaking to you. #EffectiveContent @ResultsLady

_____

_____

_____

125

If you have confusing marketing messages, you will have no clients. Keep it clear and simple. #EffectiveContentMarketing @ResultsLady

_____

_____

_____

Share the AHA messages from this book socially by going to
http://aha.pub/EffectiveContentMarketing.

Section VIII
From Content to Cash

Entrepreneurs create opportunities; content marketing creates money-making opportunities. So, turning your content into cash requires consistent daily sharing of content and consistent growth of your community. Utilize webinars and email marketing to give deeper content to help your prospect become a client.

Remember, content is the new currency of the world; you must be committed to putting out a lot of it to become successful. Keep in mind that every service-based entrepreneur has knowledge that can be turned into content to make you $$$. You just need the guts to put it out there and market it.

Watch this video: **http://aha.pub/ECMs8**.

126

Successful businesses put out a lot of content. Content is the currency of the online world. #EffectiveContentMarketing @ResultsLady

_____

_____

_____

127

Turning #ContentIntoCash requires a commitment to sharing content daily through blogs, videos & social media. #ContentMarketing @ResultsLady

_____

_____

_____

128

Add 5 people to your community every day. At the end of 1 year, you will have grown your community by 1865. #ContentToCash @ResultsLady

_____

_____

_____

129

Most people need to see someone else hit the like button — they don't want to be the first one. #BuildYourAudience @ResultsLady

---

130

Be willing to share your best stuff! It will turn from just content into $$$. #ContentToCash @ResultsLady

---

131

#Entrepreneurs create opportunity!
#ContentMarketing creates opportunity for
$$$. #ContentToCash @ResultsLady

_____

_____

_____

132

Track your #ContentMarketing metrics: shares, comments, likes! Remember what you focus on creates results. #ContentToCash @ResultsLady

_____

_____

_____

133

Make sure people are building a good relationship with you through your content. #ConnectingWithContent #EffectiveContent @ResultsLady

_____

_____

_____

134

Webinars are content. Use them to offer your prospects your product or services. #WebinarsMakeMoney #ContentToCash @ResultsLady

_____

_____

_____

135

The last paragraph of your blog is your call to action. Opt-in for a freebie, click on sales page, or take survey. #ContentToCash @ResultsLady

_____

_____

_____

136

#EmailMarketing is #ContentMarketing. Email your list several times a week. Educate them & they will buy! #ContentToCash @ResultsLady

_____

_____

_____

137

Take questions that are answers in a sales pitch, and record a video of you answering those questions. #YouHaveContent @ResultsLady

_____

_____

_____

138

Putting your #CallToAction after the 1st paragraph in your #EmailMarketing will increase your conversion. #ContentToCash @ResultsLady

---

139

On social media, the things we can measure are audience size, audience interaction, and conversion. #KnowYourNumbers @ResultsLady

---

140

Every service-based entrepreneur
has knowledge that can be turned
into content and make them $$$.
#EffectiveContentMarketing @ResultsLady

_____

_____

_____

About the Author

Michele Scism is a decisive, driven, and committed entrepreneur who helps successful business owners create passive income streams so they can start enjoying the benefits of entrepreneurship. Her business expertise has been highlighted during her speech at Harvard and on NBC, CBS, Fox, Entrepreneur.com, and Forbes.com.

Michele is the founder and CEO of Decisive Minds (https://decisiveminds.com). Decisive Minds provides detailed and actionable strategies for online and offline marketing, pricing, revenue projection, sales, team building, and many more.

AHAthat™

AHAthat makes it easy to share, author, and promote content. There are over 40,000 AHA messages™ by thought leaders from around the world that you can share in seconds for free on Twitter, Facebook, LinkedIn and Google+.

For those who want to author their own book, we have time-tested proven processes that allows you to write your AHAbook™ of 140 digestible, bite-sized morsels in eight hours or less. Once your content is on AHAthat, you have a customized link that you can use to have your fans/advocates share your content and help you grow your network.

➲ Start sharing: https://AHAthat.com

➲ Start authoring: https://AHAthat.com/Author

Michele Scism
AHAthat Author

Hey, Did You AHAthat™?

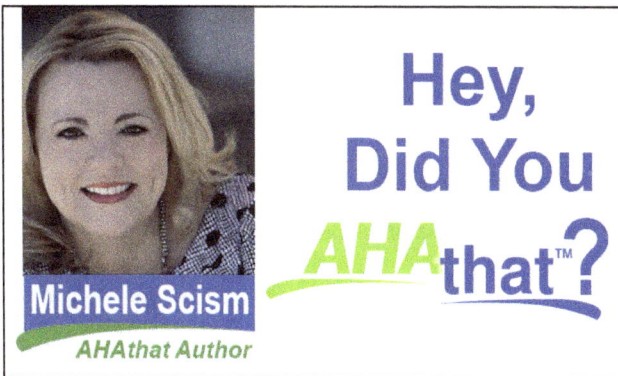

Please go directly to this book in AHAthat and share each AHAmessage socially at
http://aha.pub/EffectiveContentMarketing.

www.ingramcontent.com/pod-product-compliance
Lightning Source LLC
Chambersburg PA
CBHW071159200326
41519CB00018B/5282